The Soldier Life was in our Blood

Perry Pierik and Marcel Reijmerink

The Soldier Life was in our Blood

Karl Ullrich, the last commander of 'Wiking', a confession

Aspekt Publishers

The Soldier Life was in our Blood
© 2023 ASPEKT Publishers
Amersfoortsestraat 27, 3769 AD Soesterberg, The Netherlands
info@uitgeverijaspekt.nl - http://www.uitgeverijaspekt.nl
Cover design: Snegina Uzunova
Translation: Isabel Oomen

ISBN: 9789464870183
NUR: 680

All rights reserved. No part of this publication may be reproduced, stored in a retrieval system or transmitted in any form or by any means, electronic, mechanical, photocopying, recording or otherwise, without the prior permission of the publisher.

Table of contents

Foreword	7
Introduction	13
Hitler	15
Bad Reichenhall	21
The Childhood Years	25
The Waffen-SS	33
Der Mut der Ahnungslosen	41
The Easy Win	49
Himmler	57
Easy Rider	67
The Persecution of Jews	69
The Eastern Front	75
My Homeland	111
Karl Ullrich's Life in a Nutshell	115
Literature	119

Foreword

Hungry for wonderful stories from Europe's most recent history, we travelled to Eastern Europe in the early 1990s. Keeping an open mind (as much as possible), without prejudice and as few plans and appointments as possible. We were surprised by who and what we encountered. It resulted in wonderful conversations with diverse people from different countries. We recorded these conversations in articles for national newspapers and magazines. And so, in the summer of 1990, we accidentally ended up with Karl Ullrich, who died in 1996.

We had both just finished teacher training and university when the 'Wall' fell. A new world order was starting. For us this meant a starting point for revisiting all the issues in Europe's recent history - literally and figuratively. Our baggage was the oppressive, intellectual period of the 1980s, during which you were still regularly measured along the bar of right and wrong. If you were critical of the ANC, for instance, you were immediately pro-apartheid. If you thought the GDR was not German, not democratic and not a republic, you were on the far right of the Cold War spectrum. A tricky environment, then, to satisfy your curiosity in all sorts of topics. The 'Fall of the Wall', the completion of studies and the new life of freelance journalist were a small liberation from this world for us. And the real liberation is mainly in travelling and meeting all kinds of people in free Europe. Something that, as a result of the Cold War, seemed entirely, unimaginably far away in the 1980s.

In those years - 'it is now a quarter century later and almost unimaginable, especially for the generation studying now, it was *not done to* let the 'wrong' German side of World War II have its say'. Albert Speer's memoirs were then still accepted because he clearly confessed guilt and distanced himself from the Third Reich. But it was inconceivable and undesirable to interview Germans with a Nazi past, without open apologies on their part, and have their side of the story told. They were not ready for that. Very unfortunate, we thought (and still think). Precisely because through letting eyewitnesses of World War II speak freely, you find out how they thought and often still think. It gives you a picture of *the other side of the hill*. A unique insight into how these people thought, acted and how they still struggle with their past. Without us 'jubilantly' embracing those stories, but also without immediate harsh judgements.

With this intent, with this bias, we decided to visit Karl Ullrich - soldier, commander in SS divisions 'Totenkopf' and 'Wiking' - during our unfortunate return trip from Hungary. We did not know much more about Ullrich than what is written in the previous sentence. We knew that he had been on the Eastern Front and squeezed out one last offensive with his 'Wiking' division in Hungary at the end of the war. In retrospect, it was a historic shot in the arm. Ullrich had met Hitler and Himmler. He fought in the Blitzkrieg against Holland and France. He experienced the invasion of Poland ('Ab jetzt wird zurück geschossen') and the campaign to Russia - and back again. However, most importantly, he was ready to share his position on the annihilation of the Jews.

Ullrich spoke, we still remember, open-heartedly - with an open mind. But on one subject he was reserved. He only wanted to say something *off-the-record* about that, namely about 'camaraderie' in the post-war era. Of course, everyone knew that ex-Waffen-SS soldiers still got together after the war and got each other jobs to help each other. That solidarity runs deeply in that generation of Germans. At these - often closed - gatherings, where undoubtedly songs from the Nazi era were sung again, there were celebrities as well, Germans who achieved great fame on television during the 'Nachkriegszeit', but who certainly did not forget their comrades of old and regularly came to these gatherings of former soldiers. Likewise, Ullrich told us, Herbert Reinecker, the writer of the immensely popular TV series *Derrick* and frontline reporter with the Waffen-SS, regularly visited. 'He was and is still one of us,' Ullrich told me proudly, but also cautiously. He did not want to damage Reinecker's name and fame. Although, Reinecker was open and honest about it in his biography (which came out a few months later) - at least about his SS past, not about his post-war kinship with his old comrades.

Germans of that generation have this struggle with themselves (on the one hand knowing they were 'wrong', on the other not daring or wanting to come out) that is still unresolved. The writer Günter Grass, who passionately aspired to be the most 'good' German on earth after the war, later gave a startling confession that he had served in the Waffen-SS (August 2006). Grass further admitted later in life that Nazism was still locked inside him. As an example, he gave that, as if out of nowhere, he used to hum a happy tune from the Hitler Youth era when shaving in the morning. Nazism got under the skin of Germans (of his generation) more than they wanted to admit and talk about. That, too, did Grass admit.

Moreover, it is remarkable that Grass, as the German historian Malte Herwig writes, never wanted to admit that he signed up as a party member of Hitler's NSDAP: 'I cannot remember'. People repress what they experienced, what they did. With Grass (as well as other intellectuals of his age), this meant repressing and denying becoming an active member of the NSDAP. This was systematically denied by Grass and his intellectual contemporaries, even though it proved to be an incontrovertible fact.

For many Germans who fought on the Eastern Front, it was easier to repress, forget, and look away, erasing the atrocities of the Holocaust from their hard drive. All the soldiers must have had 'something' to do with it, but do not talk about it, deny it, condone it or downplay it. As with Grass and his 'forgotten' party membership, they do not want to remember the 'Final Solution'.

So too with Karl Ullrich. Some details he remembered extremely well. And although he talks about the Jews without holding back, he let loose little about the 'Final Solution'. Still, although he did not become a 'Gutmensch in extremis' like Grass, his memories as a soldier were more than worth listening to during our two- day visit to him in Bad Reichenhall. It gives an insight into the thought processes of SS soldiers who were 'there' from the beginning. A small goldmine for *oral history*. A goldmine because this generation of frontline soldiers is (virtually) extinct. For young historians, the witnesses of this important epoch are as far away for us in 1990 as the witnesses who lived through the Franco- German war of 1870- 1871.

In this mini-document, at least a remnant has remained worthy. A remnant of the 'big history' sharing the 'little story'. And precisely because it is the 'little story' of the 'wrong' side, which has long been hushed up, this story is a small, previously unpublished contribution to a full picture of the events, thinking and acting of World War II.

Perry Pierik
Marcel Reijmerink
Soesterberg Utrecht, July 2015

'SS-Oberführer der Waffen-SS' Ullrich

Iron drills at the Waffen-SS

Introduction

Coming from Hungary, we are forced to make a stop in southern Germany since we have problems with our car. The battery is in need of cooling. We decide to spend the night in the Bavarian town of Bad Reichenhall. We did not choose this town at random. This is where the almost 80-year-old former commander of the SS armoured division 'Wiking', Karl Ullrich, lives. Arriving at the hotel, we quickly check whether he is in the phone book. Yes, he is in it. We immediately call to ask if we can interview him in the coming days. Ullrich's health is still good. He agrees. The car trouble that has been troubling us the entire holiday might now bring us luck for once. We know it is a unique opportunity to delve into the past of a man such as this. He is one of the few SS commanders still alive. Tomorrow will be an exciting day. We are aware of that.

Karl Ullrich

Hitler

In the middle of the forest, a large wooden house stands gloomily in the shade. It is the Wolfschanze in East Prussia. 'The Führer headquarters' from where Hitler's armies and divisions receive their orders daily. Present are a large number of officers, such as Field Marshal Keitel, chief of the 'OKW', General Jodl, chief of the OKW's 'operations bureau', his assistant Warlimont, a delegate from the navy, Vice-Admiral Yoss, a representative of the 'Waffen-SS' and several more officers. They are waiting for the Führer. The officers are somewhat impatient. Perhaps this is due to the construction work, which some have jokingly described as a cross between a monastery and a concentration camp. Or is it the endless stream of disappointing news from the front about the forced German retreat east and west. Then Hitler arrives and the meeting begins. Situations on the various fronts are outlined, new martial plans discussed. The discussion cannot take too long. From Italy, Hitler's ally Benito Mussolini is expected. Hitler wants to encourage 'Il Duce' to keep supporting the German side. Suddenly, there is a huge explosion. The wooden house is badly damaged and filled with smoke. Generals lie dead on the ground, wounded shriek and cry for help. A totally dazed man emerges from the clouds of dust. His hair is scorched, his left arm hurt, his drum membranes damaged and his uniform destroyed. It is Adolf Hitler, 20 July 1944. The attack on Hitler, planned by a handful of officers and carried out by Claus von Stauffenberg, has failed.

Nine days later, a Volkswagen Kübelwagen arrives at the Wolfschanze. Inside the car is a Waffen-SS man dressed in camouflage uniform. It is 33-year-old Karl Ullrich. His car follows the winding road through the dark and damp forests. The area is full of mines and there are checkpoints everywhere. Ullrich is stopped three times by his colleagues from the 'Führer', who are even more careful than usual. Eventually Ullrich arrives, beyond the houses of Jodl, Keitel, Göring and Dr Morell, Hitler's personal physician, at the 'Führer headquarters'. It is the third time Ullrich will meet Hitler. Ullrich is led into a side room by an adjutant and the wait begins for him. It *is* a busy place, with officers walking back and forth. No wonder, there is a lot to discuss. Meanwhile, in Berlin, Major Otto Ernst Remer, commander of the 'Wach' battalion 'Großdeutschland', has put down the coup against Hitler. The 'Reichsführer-SS', Heinrich Himmler, has been given all the necessary proxies by Hitler to quell the resistance. A veritable wave of arrests takes place in the Third Reich. The conspirators are hopeless and are dragged before Roland Freisler's cruel people's court.

In addition, the attack has been a shock to soldiers at the front. Some feel it as another stab in the back and compare it to 1918, when parts of the army answered the call for revolution. Still, the German soldier of 1944 remains where he stands. Perhaps this is due to the fact that, as the later commander of the army group 'Südukraine' wrote, the German soldier, especially in the east, has long since ceased to be in the field on command. A grotesque struggle of titans took place in the east during the summer of 1941; a huge clash between two intolerant philosophies of life. In the summer of 1943, the Germans made a final attempt to turn the tide in their favour. However, this failed hopelessly. Mid 1944, soldiers realise that the preservation of the homeland will soon need to be fought for.

Ullrich, waiting for the Führer to award him the 'Eichenlaub' for great heroism, is painfully aware of all this. As battalion commander of the notorious Waffen-SS divi-

SS-Grenadiers

Anti-tank Artillery

sion 'Totenkopf', he knows like no other the 'Älltag' of the front. Typical of this are the battered ranks of 'Totenkopf', which were replenished with several thousand young and inexperienced recruits from the homeland a few weeks ago. How long these will last at the front is the question.

Otto Günsche, Hitler's adjutant, appears out of nowhere in front of the battalions of 'Totenkopf'. Ullrich is taken to a small room. Then suddenly Hitler appears, and Ullrich is startled. Hitler has become an old man. He walks up to Ullrich, pins the Eichenlaub on him and shakes his hand. Hitler's blue eyes look straight at Ullrich, whom feels no hypnotic effect, as he has heard from others. 'Maybe I have already experienced too much at the front,' he declares after the war.

As Hitler continues to hold his hand, he asks: 'What are you doing right now?' This is a difficult question, because Ullrich has just been transferred and hesitates. However, the Reichsführer-SS Himmler rescues him from this embarrassing situation.

'Ullrich leads the 'Totenkopf' Division, mein Führer'.

Hitler: 'How strong?'

Ullrich, who has only led the division for a single day as a deputy, has no idea about this. But again, Himmler comes to his rescue: '18,000 men, mein Führer'.

Ullrich knows this is a outright lie, but remains silent. Hitler nods and continues to look at Ullrich sternly, saying: 'The world is round and what is below will rise above'. After this, Hitler turns and walks away. Ullrich is left confused and alone, the 'Eichenlaub' hanging over the 'Ritterkreuz'.

Bad Reichenhall

At our leisure, we drive through Bad Reichenhall once more. The next day we will visit Karl Ullrich here. The houses there are big. The richness of Bavarian life radiates everywhere. We do not see any young people. The place is full of elderly people who come to visit the hospitals and calm. Judging by the questioning faces of the Germans, they do not understand what we are doing here. After all, we are the only foreigners in Bad Reichenhall. This arouses suspicion. Nevertheless, we are well received at our hotel. After all, we speak good German. Dutch people always speak their languages well, people say. We are the Chinese of Europe.

We have not yet unpacked our suitcases when Frau Huber, our hostess, starts explaining elaborately where we can best eat Bavarian-style. We listen obligingly. Outside the hotel, we look at each other and automatically walk to the Greek restaurant. It is the only foreign restaurant in Bad Reichenhall. Despite the sweltering heat, which takes away all appetite beforehand, the Greek meat dish still tastes good. We have to admit that the Bavarian beer goes down well, too. As we have an early appointment with Ullrich for the next day, we decide to walk back to the hotel immediately after dinner.

We can hear the music from afar. A Bavarian brass band is playing German tunes. For the birthday of the hotel owner, as it turns out. He is "Ehrenvorsitzender" of this wind band. All Bavarian men over the age of five are 'Ehrenvorsitzender' of something. Fortunately, playing on these hopeless instruments is quickly discontinued. Otherwise we would have had to file a noise complaint with the Bavarian police.

The next day, the car does not work. The battery is broken. There is always something when you are in Germany. So we start walking. The distance is certainly not easy. Finally, we arrive in the street where Ullrich lives, completely exhausted. At the street corner, we stop to rest for a while. Today's youth no longer has any condition. That much is certain. We walk the last metres down the street to Ullrich's house, and our eyes enjoy a feast. Some houses are even bigger than others. We read the hypertrophied nameplates; they are all houses of doctors and engineers. Germans still love titles.

Ullrich is an engineer too, as we know from the phone book. Suddenly, we are in front of a nursing home for the elderly. This must be where Ullrich lives. And yes, he is already waiting for us outside. He slowly rises from his chair and welcomes us with the words: 'Ah, da sind die Historiker aus Holland'. The woman sitting next to him nods kindly but aloof. She must be thinking, what are these sweaty weirdos doing here? However, we stoically follow Ullrich, who brings us into a cool conversation room.

We are alone. In the corner of the room is a slide screen. For the rest, there is a large table. However, only one thing interests us at that moment: the chairs. We quickly sit down. After exchanging a few pleasantries, we begin the interview.

The Childhood Years

Ullrich is now 79 years old, but his eyes are still sharp. He wears a blue Lacoste T-shirt. So he goes with the fashion. Only his breathing is a bit heavy. Still, we hardly notice that because we are still gasping for breath ourselves.

'I grew up in Bad Kissingen. My father, called Leopold, was a civil servant in finance. I also went to high school in Bad Kissingen. However, my father and mother, whose name was Barbara, wanted me to get a good education. She sent me to Würzburg, where I studied to become an engineer. I was always active in the student associations there. The most popular leisure activity was fencing. I did a lot of fencing.'

Hence that scar on your face?

'Yes, that happened at a duel. We were not protected by masks then as we are now.'

Dangerous time, even then?

Karl Ullrich as officer with the pioneers

'Ah what. I fought only four real duels. The best fencers came from Germany, did you know that? Even today. But it was one of the most beautiful times of my life. I only dream about it. I can still remember the days when we went out in Würzburg on Saturday afternoons with four and a half marks in the trouser pocket. A wonderful time.'

When were you done dreaming?

'When I went to work at the MAN-factory in Nuremberg in 1927. I came there as an intern. You were not accepted as an apprentice by anyone. Not by the management because you were still too young and not by the workers either. They knew that one day you would become their boss, upstairs in the office. I have always regretted that attitude.'

What did you learn there?"

'Two things. The craft and the politics. Let us start with the first.
　You worked from 6.30am to five o'clock at night. You were constantly behind the workbench. This is where I learnt the technical side of the trade. But I also learnt what it is to be a worker. As workers, you had no legal status whatsoever. 'Grüss Gott' you were not allowed to say. Then you would be kicked out. You had to work as many as 54 hours a week. That was a terrible life. You did not see any daylight. I had sympathy for the workers' demands then.'

And so then you joined the Communist Party?

'No, of course not. I have never had anything to do with those gingers.'

Why not?

'I will tell you. I attended a 1st May celebration in Nuremberg. A worker, with whom I was living at the time, invited me to attend that meeting. It was on a Sunday. A day when workers were free. Since it was only allowed to celebrate the 1st of May in Germany on a day off, i.e. a Sunday. If you did not do that on a day off, you were fired. Ridiculous. Anyway, we went to that meeting and a communist spoke there. He was a 'Reichstag' delegate and his name was Simon. Dressed in a far too nice black suit, he spoke of 'we proletarians'.

How could he say that? The workers who had never seen sun looked deathly pale. They were skinny because of too hard work and poor nutrition and hygiene. In the factories, for instance, there were not even washing facilities. Yet you did not hear the saloon socialist talking about that. He only talked about the world proletariat. What did those workers get out of that? Nothing, right? That communist, though, looked tanned and plump. That man did not speak the workers' language.'

The National Socialists did?

'Yes. Those spoke the language of the workers. They knew what they were talking about. They understood that the German workers wanted to go to the barricades to stand up for their rights.'

What else did the National Socialists offer?

'They didn't think internationally. I thought that was a triumph. Finally a party that stood up for our national interests.'

And beyond that?

'Furthermore, the National Socialists protected the militia, reinstated it.'

Marcel Reijmerink in conversation with Karl Ullrich

Why did you think that was important? You were an engineer-to-be, not a soldier, right?

'I come from a military family. My grandfather fought in Africa. The soldier's life was in our blood. Also in mine. I was extremely annoyed by the leftist newspapers that blamed the military for everything. Then the NSDAP came along and I thought that was a fine counterbalance to that leftist chatter.'

When did you become a member?

'In 1931, I became a member. Number 717000. I immediately joined the SA. In 1932, I joined the SS as member number 31,000.'

Why the switch?

'The SA was too boring. Too dull.'

But did the SA not see battle quite a few times?

'I was not looking for that. I was looking for camaraderie. I found that in the SS. Many students joined the SS and that camaraderie of those days is still there.'

But by no means did all students join the SS? 'No, certainly not.'

Was there much hatred and envy?

'Ah, that wasn't so bad. I had a fellow student called Kamsch, who was a communist. We had a lot of discussions. Nothing more. He once said in 1932: 'This summer you can come with me to Russia. Up to the border we will go with by bicycle. From there, the Russians pay for everything. For you too, even if you are from the SS. I guarantee it.' When the holidays arrived and I asked him when we were going next, he claimed he had turned down the Russians' offer. Outright lie, of course. But I liked him. He really believed in the paradise called Russia. Ah well, he was dreaming.'

You were dreaming too, were you not?

'Then no more.'

Ullrich is in good spirits. He smiles kindly. He is happy to have been able to tell a bit about his childhood. However, we are already thinking about the next topic: the Polish campaign. How did those Germans manage to cross Poland so quickly? Would they not have grown tired of that? In any case, it would not have been something for us. We can already feel our calves after walking a bit in Bad Reichenhall. We have no 'Ausdauer'. Those Germans must have. That much about the Polish campaign is clear to us.

The Waffen-SS

Ullrich was with the Waffen-SS. A loaded term. Anyone who takes the trouble to browse through the existing literature immediately comes across this issue. The Waffen-SS formed the armed branch of Himmler's notorious SS empire. Its soldiers had the same uniforms and ranks as the general SS, which was responsible for the concentration camps. This had a bad impact on the image of the Waffen-SS. Thereby, many soldiers of the Waffen-SS, most of whom were volunteers, were ideo- logically aligned with the NSDAP. Finally, as a redundant fourth army unit, the Waffen-SS was essentially a competitor to the army. All these factors contributed to the Waffen-SS becoming a controversial organisation. Tensions rose even more because of the disappointing results at the front. Hitler, always suspicious of the land forces' 'Junkers', relied more and more on his Waffen-SS. From the summer of 1943, there was no offensive without the Waffen-SS playing a central role. To this end, the Waffen-SS was increasingly built into a mass army, partly by hundreds of thousands of volunteers from all over Europe. This did cause a decline in quality, because the

March of the 'Totenkopf' division in Russia

Karl Ullrich with Hellmuth Becker (left), commander of the 'Totenkopf' division

Ullirch, middle, with binoculars at the 'Totenkopf' division

Karl Ullrich as 'SS-Standartenführer'

Karl Ullrich

Ullrich in converstation with SS-general Gille

Ullrich as regiment commander

Ullrich with a fur hat, Eastern Front

reinforcements increasingly consisted of soldiers recruited involuntarily. In Hungary in 1945, it finally came to a break between Hitler and the Waffen-SS. Given the disappointing results of the Waffen-SS, Hitler decided to remove the 'Aermelstreifen' with name of the division. In doing so, he followed the example of Frederick the Great, whom he admired, and who also did not shy away from taking away failing units' badges of honour. The disappointment in the Waffen-SS over so much ingratitude was enormous. In the final days, therefore, the Waffen-SS deserted to the same extent as the army.

Der Mut der Ahnungslosen

The streets are filled with frenzied citizens. In the middle of the road, endless rows of soldiers march past, followed by a sea of flags and banners. With eerie precision, the boots keep pace. In front of the steps, the men turn their faces towards the 'Führer'. It is 20 April 1939, Hitler's fiftieth birthday. In Hitler's eyes, this is an advanced age. He is in a hurry; he is at the height of his power after the liberation of Austria and the non-violent reckoning with Czechoslovakia. Yet his ambitions go further. A hate campaign against Poland has begun in the press. To the German-Polish forces. Among them also units of the Waffen-SS, at the time still referred to as the 'Verfügungstruppen'. At this moment, these were still only small units, no more than 25,000 men, spread across the divisions of the land forces.

Karl Ullrich is also on the German-Polish border in 'Oberschlesien'. Ullrich is commander of the third company of the pioneer battalion of the 'SS Verfügungs-division', a logical position given his training. Like everyone else, he is tense and wonders what the future will bring.

His company is stationed in a forest area. Ullrich's curiosity eventually wins out over his obedience. Despite an explicit ban, in late August 1939, Ullrich decides to cautiously make his way to the German-Polish border to get a glimpse of his possible future adversary.

Karl Ullrich sits opposite us, he begins to smile, his eyes light up and twinkle. Despite his advanced age, Ullrich makes an intelligent and lively impression and, above all, an opinionated one. He is not the man to let words be put in his mouth. He already had this trait back then: 'Of course I wanted to know what was 'los war' there,' grins Ullrich, 'if I had to attack there I had to know what it looked like. I sneaked to the border carefully and several hundred metres before the border I unexpectedly encountered a perimeter guard. We startled each other and he immediately said in a loud tone, 'Do you not know that what you are doing now is strictly forbidden?' I explained my plan to him and was able to walk on.

Near the border, I accidentally stumbled upon a hunter's lookout in a tree, a great way to get an overview of the landscape. I climbed up to the top and looked to the east. There lay Poland. As far as I could see, there was forest. This did not make me much wiser and I climbed down. There, to my surprise, I found an army artillery officer who had come for the same reason I had. 'There is nothing to see', I told the officer who, however, still climbed up to ascertain this. Meanwhile, I walked back to my company at my leisure. I was hardly a hundred metres from the observation post when a shot rang out.

My breath stopped and I turned around. Behind me, the artillery officer quickly climbed out of the lookout and shouted: 'I am being shot at'. I realised now that the war was closer than it appeared.'

That incident was followed by a 'Riesenbefehl' on the German side, prohibiting any further explorations undertaken on his own. Yet Ullrich was not discouraged so easily. He borrowed a straw hat and overalls from a farmer and set about mowing near the German-Polish border. Ullrich is now close to the small bridge that he will have to capture in the event of war. At first glance, it does not look like it is without mines. The two Polish soldiers are day dreaming a bit. The weather is nice and the country looks peaceful. The war now seems far away again.

However, on 24 August 1939, the tension is mounting. Endless tirades about the murder of 'Volksdeutschen', the German-speaking minorities in Poland, sound from the radio equipment. The order to mobilise comes. Yet, on the night of 25 to 26 August, calm returned. 'We were very happy,' says Ullrich. 'Of course we did not want a war either'. A few days later, however, a new mobilisation order followed. The unit is taken up to near the border. Here the long wait began. 'We asked what it would be like to fight a war. What would await us? A Hauptmann of the 'Flak' of our age, about 27 or 28 who had fought in the Spanish Civil War with the 'Condor Legion', told us his experiences. We were all huddled together, a candle in the middle. I felt nervous.'

At five in the morning, the pioneers must be ready. On the Polish side of the border, tree fences are clearly visible. 'Suddenly we are startled. A heavy hum is heard in the distance, slowly approaching, dots appear on the horizon, then they fly over; our 'Luftwaffe', menacing and massive. War is a fact. The tension in all of us discharges with such an ally. It is a great feeling'. Ullrich gathers his pioneers and penetrates the border. As quickly as possible, the roadblocks are removed and the mines cleared. But before reaching the little bridge near the village, it goes up in the air. Ullrich has his first wounded.

Militarily and economically, Germany was ready to wage war against Poland in 1939, but not yet strong enough for a conflict in the West. The Germans had 102 divisions and 4,300 aircraft at their disposal and out-

Karl Ullrich's inspection

numbered the Poles both numerically and qualitatively. Nevertheless, the German army is hastily deployed and expanded in breadth rather than depth. Indeed, it lacks skilled men and all kinds of materials. The armoured weapon is also only in its infancy. The campaign against Poland is only a pseudo-Blitzkrieg.

Ullrich: 'We were ill-prepared for war. Take my pioneer company. We had no radio equipment and what was worse, I did not even have any bridge-building equipment. Now that the Poles had blown up that bridge, there was nothing left but to improvise. We made an emergency bridge from wooden planks. Looking back, it was a ridiculous situation. But we possessed 'der Mut der Ahnungslosen' and carried out our orders with enthusiasm and to the best of our ability.

Polish prisoners of war

Nonetheless, the situation for the Poles is hopeless. The Polish air force is largely destroyed on the ground. The land forces are clumsily deployed along the long border. Natural obstacles are not exploited. On 17 September 1939, Warsaw is surrounded and the end of the war is in sight. Ullrich's pioneers are positioned before Warsaw in the final days. Ullrich forms the far left wing of the German attack. Ullrich's face twitches, looking as if he is in pain. 'This was a very bad position,' he says. 'In front of us the big grey residential barracks of Warsaw and in the flank the Poles who attacked unabated. On the last day of the Polish campaign, they were still attacking across the flatlands at five in the afternoon. 'We lay in positions and mowed them down piece by piece. Not one got through. The field was littered with dead and wounded. I lost at least five men. It was a 'hässlicher Krieg'. From an army major, his name was Hallerleben, I heard of the

Polen, 1939, 'Volksdeutschen' welcome the invading troops

Polish capitulation, just before our planned storming of the blocks. I was greatly relieved and ordered everyone to remain motionless, as there was still shooting.'

A day later, by two in the afternoon, calm returns. All you hear now is the groans of the wounded lying on the no man's land, unable to be helped. The soldiers sit close together in trenches and craters. Then suddenly a Polish officer appears with a white flag. The Polish officer asks for permission to take the wounded to safety, which he receives. The Polish officer immediately stays with the Germans and Ullrich expresses to him his regret that Poland lost the war. 'Lost how?' asks the astonished Polish officer. 'Do you not know yet that the British have landed at your back?' Ullrich is baffled. The Poles seemingly have no knowledge of the real situation. England and France may have declared war on Germany, but in the

The Polish army was no match for the 'Wehrmacht'

west 'Sitzkrieg' reigns, an apathetic time that will last until May 1940. The units of the 'Yerfügungsdivision' are assembled in Czechoslovakia to be developed into a proper division.

The Easy Win

The border between the tiny Netherlands and the German Empire is three hundred kilometres long. It is impossible for the small Dutch army to divide this long border, which is why the Dutch commander-in-chief, General Winkelman, entrenched his troops in a series of water lines running one hundred to the south. These bear names like IJssel Line, Maas Line, Peel-Raamstelling and other lines that will have to defend the fortress of Holland. The Germans are aware that the rivers, canals and inundations play an important role in the Dutch defence plan. Therefore, the Germans decide on an unorthodox attack. The paratroopers and airborne troops will have to take the Dutch bridges by surprise and the land forces will have to reach them as quickly as possible. Logically, motorised troops will play an important role in this.

Proportionally, the Waffen-SS is a major part of this, with the 'Leibstandarte Adolf Hitler' under the leadership of the ex-butcher and Hitler loyalist Sepp Dietrich and the 'SS-Verfügungsdivision'. The latter division, to which Ullrich was assigned, was led by the one-eyed Paul Hausser.

Although the German paratroopers and airborne troops suffer heavy losses, the campaign against the Netherlands is still a great German success. The 'Leibstandarte' advanced as much as 110 kilometres on the first day! The 'SS-Verfügingsdivision', working together with the 9th Armoured Division within the XXVIth Army Corps, also successfully captured the railway bridge near Gennep, the only bridge on the Meuse to fall into German hands intact.

Ullrich smiles at us when we ask how the Dutch fought then: 'Ah, they didn't want a war anyway,' he says, gesturing with his hands up. 'At the beginning, there was no opposition at all. We simply wandered into Holland. We came to a badly blown swing bridge and I rushed forward in my motorbike with sidecar to give my pioneers orders. But here we encountered the first Dutch resistance. With machine guns, the Dutch sprayed from the other bank the dyke on which we were riding.

Our motorbike came under heavy fire. I gestured to my driver to turn back quickly. I got out and through the ditches I snuck forward.'

Ullrich is really starting to have fun with his story now. Maybe due to the fact that we are Dutch. 'There was a Dutchman with a cannon and he had it specifically

SS-general Paul Hausser

aimed at me. Every shot was aimed at me. He seemingly had plenty of ammunition. Meanwhile, the shots were approaching me by the minute and I understood that I had to get back to the bulk of my company that was behind me. In front of my men I jumped up and ran. And I wanted to run, I assure you! I even jumped over a six metre wide inundation in one go!

We look at each other for a moment. Clearly, the world lost a great athlete in Ullrich.

'Later we managed to get to the other bank but, of course, that brought losses. As a pioneer, I made everything happen as quickly as possible. We played an important role in the watery Netherlands. I still remember one day. Together with a sub-officer I was reconnoitring at the front. I told him to keep walking right behind me because of the landmines.

I had a good nose for these things and I was sure to get around them. Suddenly, a huge explosion sounded behind us. A young soldier from the regiment 'Deutschland' had stepped on a mine. I ran towards it. Both his legs had been torn off, from his waist down everything was gone. He was screaming. But what could we do? A 'Sani' rushed to him but he, too, was looking hopeless.'

There is silence for a while. We too know not what to say. Ullrich looks from one to the other. 'Schrecklich' he says and shrugs. 'But yes, it was war'.

Karl Ullrich and his pioneer troops

German Wehrmacht and disabled French tank, summer, 1940

In the final days of the war with the Netherlands, Ullrichs pioneers were deployed in the province of Zeeland, during which they also came into combat contact with General Henri Giraud's French troops of the 7th Army, who wanted to come to the aid of the Dutch on 11 May 1940. On 14 May, after the bombing of Rotterdam, the Dutch resistance collapses. Ullrich disarms a Dutch cavalry unit in Harderwijk. 'The Dutch were good soldiers. I have experienced them in the German military service of the European volunteer division 'Wiking'. But these guys did not want to fight any more at all and were happy to hand in their weapons. Even though, partly due to their colonial experience, they were better trained than us.'

Then the 'Verfügungsdivision' is deployed in France. Ullrich now keeps smiling at a stretch. With this, he confirms one of the simplest military manuals: as long as it goes forward, morale is good. 'When we arrived in France it had all already happened. Those French had stupidly deployed their tanks, scattered along the front, instead of building them into divisions. They had plenty of them, and of good quality too! Now the French were running ahead of us and we advanced all the way to the Swiss border. There was no stopping us. The French did not want to fight at all. We had done it in no time!'

Disabled 'Char B1', 1940

Capitulation French troops, summer, 1940

We were both amazed at how easily the west field trip was handled. It was seemingly all that simple. But the war will change when we come to talk about another era, Operation 'Barbarossa', the German invasion of the Soviet Union.

Himmler

We stop the interview to take a break. There is no sign of fatigue on Ullrich's part. We still look sweaty. Ullrich walks out onto the balcony. He shows us the beautiful, wide panorama of the Bavarian mountains that he gets to see every day. The sky is clear blue but still a nasty cloud hangs between the mountains. The environment is also hollowing out in Bavaria. 'Look over there'. Ullrich points. We follow his index finger. 'Behind there is Hitler's Obersalzberg. The Berghof, the eagle's nest.' He points us to a mountain that is terribly high. 'If you want to walk up the Obersalzberg you have to take a 24% slope', he continues.

'Walking?' We protest bewildered. 'We will take the car.'

'Yes, but your car is broken and you will not get mine. Well, there is not much left to see anyway. The Americans blew up the entire Berghof after the war. Everything! There are only some bunkers and some loose stones. Do you know what they have put up now? A hotel. An American hotel, named after General Walker, who was the first to arrive on the Oberslalzberg. The hotel looks like hell. American arogance. You can question Nazi architecture. I admit that. But this hotel is much uglier. Go and have a look. Then you can also look at that awful sign at the entrance of the hotel, which says: 'Sie können auch in D-Marken zahlen'. It is no longer German territory. They should never have blown up the Berghof.'

-Yes, but otherwise it will become a pilgrimage site for Nazi devotees, will it not?

'You then have to take measures against that. They can do that, right?

That no Germans are allowed upstairs?

Ullrich paces back and forth. Pondering. He rubs his fingers over the scar on his chin. He is silent.

Have you ever met any of the top people of the Third Reich besides Hitler?

'Yes, Himmler.'

What did you think of him?

'With Himmler I got on well. He was just too idealistic. He was far away from us. He was not a soldier, not like us. Himmler actually had different thoughts about the SS than we soldiers had. But even in a hundred years, people will speak positively about Himmler.'

Heinrich Himmler

But Himmler was a race extremist, was he not?

'Yes, in that respect he was an idiot.'

When did you first meet Himmler?

'That was in 1941. I was then in the Kessel of Demjansk and got a holiday. My friend from the 'Junkerschule' Werner Grothmann, had meanwhile become Himmler's adjutant. He advised me to go to the 'Führer headquarters' when I got some time off. So I did. When I reported, however, Grothmann was not there. But suddenly I heard someone shouting from Himmler's special train: 'Hey Ulli. What are you doing here?' I turned around and saw someone with a big red head. That was Diefenbacher, the man who

'Ullrich, ein Bier!' Karl Ullrich in conversation with historian Perry Pierik

*Ullrich appeared before Himmler in uniform.
'That works with the Reichsführer'*

Demjansk shield

Soldiers from the 'Totenkopf' division, in the 'Kessel' of Demjansk

Russian farmers are questioned by soldiers from the Waffen-SS

Soviet illustrations about the battle in the Demjansk area

had also educated me at the 'Junkerschule'. I was immediately given all sorts of things to eat and drink. I had my beard shaved and my hair cut. I could even watch a film if I wanted. In the evening I was allowed to eat at Himmler's table. Only my uniform was covered in Russian mud and shit. 'That doesn't matter', Diefenbacher reassured me, 'something like that does well with Himmler'. So in the evening I sat at Himmler's table. Lamers sat there as well. Himmler was very obliging. He asked what I wanted to drink. I did not have to think long about that: 'Ein frisches Bier, mein Reichsführer'. 'Ullrich, beer,' Himmler roared immediately. But it was unpalatable. It was 'Kriegsbier'. I said, 'Reichsführer, surely this is not beer!' Himmler smiled and handed me a glass of French red wine.'

You just said that Himmler was not actually a soldier. Did you not discuss military matters with him then?

'Himmler was always curious about small, not unimportant details. He asked me whether the brackets on the rifle trigger were wide enough for the thick-gloved finger to pass through. I said this was indeed a problem. Himmler then immediately made sure that the brackets of the trigger were made wider.'

You had no quarrel with Himmler?

'No, on the contrary. He was very kind. And listened attentively. After that first meeting, he sent me on holiday. I was allowed to go wherever I wanted to go. He paid for everything. Then I decided to go on holiday to Bavaria

Demjansk signpost

with my wife. In Bavaria back then, you could eat and drink well and a lot.'

So you harbour no resentment against Himmler?

'Well, that's to say. He should never have committed suicide. He should have served his prison sentence. Never should have been allowed to bite through the capsule. I was very disappointed about that. About Hitler's death, I was not disappointed. Hitler had fallen. They had killed Hitler anyway. Himmler should never have killed himself.'

Easy rider

In the afternoon, we leave Ullrich at two o'clock to continue our interview the next morning. Now we will first repair our car. We declined Ullrich's offer to have our car towed by him. Visiting a garage seems safer to us. After half an hour, we can take our car to Berchtesgaden, visit the Berghof. We follow the sign Obersalzberg and suddenly we are on a 24% slope. We cannot go back. We sit all the way back in our car seats. This is pretty much how Neil Armstrong must have sat when he was shot to the moon. At last we stand in front of the hotel general Walker. The sign that you can pay with German marks is still there. We cannot suppress a smile. We walk around the area a bit aimlessly. Everything is gone. Blown up, as Ullrich said. A whole history in tatters. Stupid Americans, we swear. Disappointed, we drive back to Bad Reichenhall.

The only entertainment in the town is the cinema. There even turns out to be a really good film running there: Easy Rider. Two motorcyclists are looking for their freedom, for their way of life without wanting to harm other people's lives. We are in the theatre with four other people. They soon leave the auditorium while the film is only halfway through. We, however, are enthralled. Impressed, we leave the cinema. We walk through Bad Reichenhall and keep seeing the same houses with the same gardens and flowers. Everything looks alike here. Everything. No one is out of place. Actually, we are the Easy Riders of Bad Reichenhall. Two eccentric figures, like in the film, two anarcho-liberal historians who can do nothing but read and write books. Apart from that, we are not suited to anything else. That seems to radiate from us. If we are shot here, like Peter Fonda and Dennis Hopper in the film, no one will help us. No one. They will draw the curtains and turn on the TV. As long as everything goes well with themselves and their peers, they do not care about anything. They call that camaraderie. It was the same with the Jews. They did not belong either. Nothing has changed. Noting. Only a facade of even greater civility has been erected.

As in Gerard Reve's novels, the sky suddenly turned grey and a drizzly rain fell on our bare arms. The wind has turned chilly. For the first time during our trip, we long for the Netherlands.

The Persecution of Jews

On the second day, Ullrich is even more generous than the previous one. He seems to enjoy being able to tell his story to young people. We are somewhat timid and tense. After all, we want to start right away with the most heavily charged subject of the Nazi era: the persecution of the Jews.

Victims of the Holocaust

Bad Reichenhall in 1945, heavily damaged

Hitler with whip at Königssee

How do you look back on the deportations of Jews?

'That was terrible. Embarrassing. In Bad Kissingen, our dentist and GP were Jewish. Friendly people. Once, when I visited our GP and he heard I was with the 'SS', he said, 'Karl, are you with them too?' But our fight against the Jews was not against them as individuals.'

What then?

'It was a percentage issue for us. There were far too many Jewish historians, lawyers, dentists and so on.

They were in control. They overdid everything. They were too zealous. But we did not quarrel with them. They declared war on us in 1933. We did not. I was not an anti- Semite. But I simply did not like them. Nobody liked them.'

Is the war against the Jews over now? 'No. The Jews determine everything now too.'

How then?

'They still hold all the power. Do you know the Swiss anti-Semite Dr Wahl? People have blocked his bankaccount so he can no longer receive money. They do that because he is an anti-Semite.'

What did you know about the deportations when you were at the front?

Berghof

'Nothing. When I came back I heard about it. About all those millions who were supposedly gassed. But what is true about it? Can you tell me? Do you know how many Jews perished at Auschwitz? Really not four million! The Poles removed the sign there that said four million Jews were gassed. Four million, that is impossible! In Dachau, too, they removed the signs. No Jew was gassed there. So much is lied about the persecution of Jews. Sooner or later some of the truth has to be known, right? Anyway, even if only a thousand Jews were gassed, that is still too many. Too hideous.'

We read a document in which you enquired how many Jews perished in all the camps at the archieves in Bad Arolsen (47 million archives, six houses filled with paper). According to this archieve, these were 271,000 registered Jews and countless unregistered Jews who perished.

'You see, not four million.'

- But then you forget the unregistered Jews. Like so many Germans, you fought for ideals that ended in terrible apocalyptic events. Were you able to cope with that?

The silence is painful. We expect Ullrich to bid us go away. But Ullrich sighs, says nothing and shuffles back and forth on his chair a bit. He remains silent. It takes a while before we can continue our interview.

The Eastern Front

On 22 June 1941, the greatest showdown since the outbreak of World War II began: the Russian Campaign. The Germans have amassed 129 divisions between the Baltic Sea and the Black Sea, making an early assault on the Soviet Union. During the campaign, the importance of the Waffen-SS increases rapidly. Initially, it is only a handful of divisions, such as the 'Leibstandarte Aldolf', 'Das Reich', 'Totenkopf' and others. But as more setbacks occur, Hitler increasingly relies on the Waffen-SS.

Just before the Russia Campaign, Ullrich is transferred from the 'Das Reich' division (the former 'SS- Verfügungsdivision') to the 3rd SS division 'Totenkopf'. 'Totenkopf' is a unit viewed with a certain distrust by the army. This is not least due to the fact that the unit is commanded by Theodor Eicke, former commander of concentration camp Dachau, near Munich, as well as by the fact that many soldiers of the division are former concentration camp guards. The division is the ghost child of Eicke, a controversial figure. Eicke was born on 17 October 1892 in Alsace-Lorraine, the son of a

Theodor Eicke managed to convince Himmler of his usefulness

railway official. After serving in the trenches from 1914-1918, Eicke started a career in the police. But due to his waywardness and negative attitude towards the Weimar Republic, he was dismissed.

However, the IG Farben concern gives him another chance. Here, Eicke was put in charge of corporate espionage. Again, he lost this job because of his political activities, as Eicke had been a member of the NSDAP since 1928 and a member of the SS since 1930, and in connection with a number of bombings, he was forced to move abroad.

On his return, the party is the only thing Eicke has left in life. 'Rücksichtslos' he fights his way to the top. A competitor he threatens with violence. This goes too far for Himmler and Eicke's party career seems to end when he disappears into a psychiatric clinic.

But Eicke is a fighter, manages to convince the impressionable 'Reichsführer' Himmler of his usefulness and makes a come-back. Thanks to his ruthlessness in the face of enemies of the regime, his prestige quickly increases and he works his way up to 'Inspekteur der Konzentrationslager und Leiter der SS-Wachverbände'. From these and other units, Eicke establishes the 'Totenkopf' division and begins a military career.

Ullrich has never heard of Eicke at the moment he arrives at 'Totenkopf'. As Ullrich reports to divisional headquarters, he suddenly hears a heavy voice behind

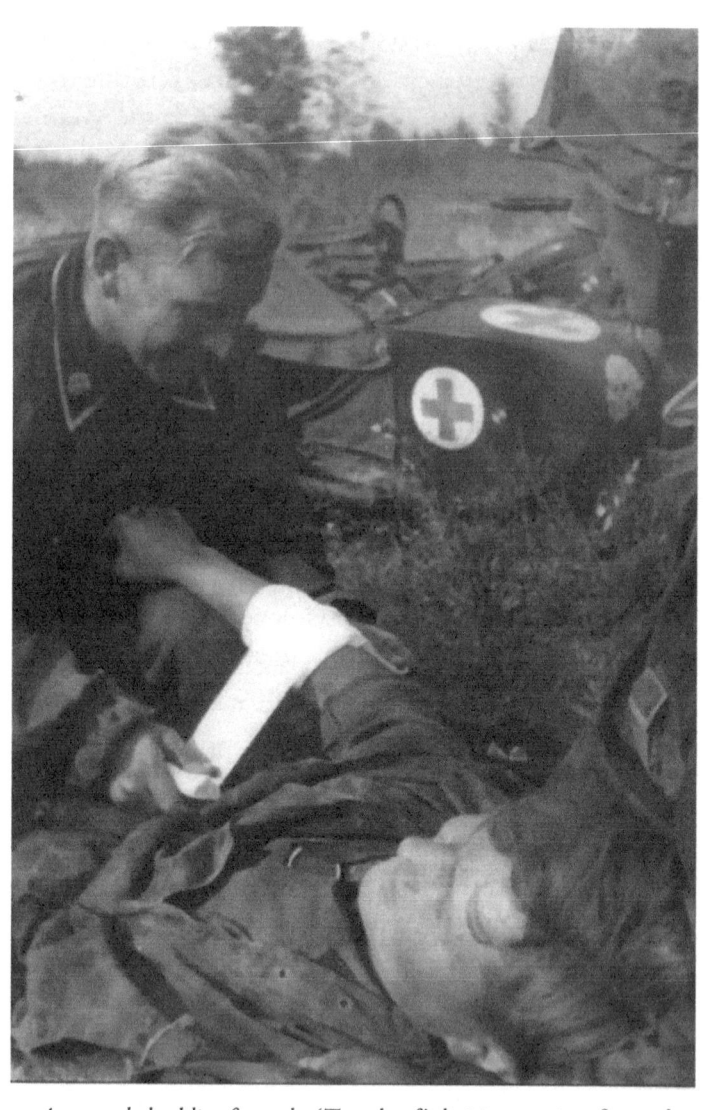

A wounded soldier from the 'Totenkopf' division receives first aid

him, asking: 'So, do we know each other?' Ullrich turns around and sees Eicke standing with a pipe in his mouth. 'No, Gruppenführer,' Ullrich replies.'

Ullrich gets to know Eicke as a 'toller Mann'.

'Eicke may not have been a great strategist, but if something was going on at the front, he was always there. It was better to have someone like that than a commander who was just sitting behind the front looking at the maps. I remember well when we broke through the Stalin line, suddenly Russian fighter planes, Ratatas, appeared and shelled us. I was walking on a mud road at that time. I hated lying down here but had no choice. As I splashed down, I heard a loud, hoarse laugh behind me. I looked back and saw Eicke right behind me also lying in the mud. His entire uniform was soaked, but it did not seem to bother him.

He asked, 'Pionierführer, what are you doing out front here?' I told him I wanted to be in front, because my pioneers had a lot of work to do. 'Five thousand marks' roared Eicke's voice and away he was again. Five thousand marks, what did he mean? My adjutant gave the solution to the riddle. As KZ commander, Eicke ran a canteen where soldiers could buy all sorts of things. A profit was made there, of course, and when Eicke set up the 'Totenkopf' division he took that cash with him. As a result, children of fallen soldiers could get a savings account and units that tried very hard could get a bonus.

Ullrich starts laughing, clearly proud of this anecdote.

'Smoking break' at the Front

'Eicke was very pleased and gave us five thousand marks which we spent well. Of course Eicke got in trouble for taking the cash. But he did not care about any of that. He was far too stubborn for that. Eicke saw himself as a rival to Sepp Dietrich, the best-known Waffen-SS officer. When he heard that Sepp had his 'Leibstandarte' carrying the 'Siegrunen' on both sides on the collar (the SS tokens), Eicke immediately wanted 'Totenkopf' to henceforth also no longer wear any rank signs, just the 'Totenkopf'.'

Despite the fact that Ullrich already knew quite a few people from 'Totenkopf' through the 'Junkerschule' and his experiences at 'Reich', it was still quite a transition. 'At 'Reich' they were all young soldiers. 'Totenkopf' was an older division. For me as a pioneer, this was only beneficial. I now had more well-trained artisans. Part of the initial successes of 'Totenkopf' can be explained by the fact that the division was somewhat older. But in the course of the war we suffered heavy losses and this advantage was lost. In addition, 'Totenkopf' was a different division politically. We felt we were the more conscious National Socialists, but we were?'

The Russia Campaign is difficult from the start. 'Totenkopf' is part of Army Group North, Hoepner's Armoured Group 4. Initially, the division, together with the 269th Infantry Division, forms the reserve. As the army group invades the Baltic States, the new war for 'Totenkopf' immediately starts dramatically. 'Some forty

Karl Ullrich with Otto Baum

Soviet troops attack

men from the scout division fell into Russian hands and were slaughtered: eyes gouged out, genitals cut off. It was horrible. And to think that in the Baltic States it was not so bad. In the Russian area, things got worse. The division had a hard time.

'Eicke had had to build the unit all by himself from scratch and the equipment had been dragged from everywhere. Thus we had many Czech weapons at our disposal, which of course was not an advantage. Fortunately, this changed over the course of the war.'

On the way to Leningrad, the division encountered the Stalin line. 'General Erich von Manstein, who incidentally could make his dachshund do the Hitler salute, had told us that this line was nothing.' Ullrich sits up straight and his voice rings loudly through the room: 'Armoured turrets the Russians had there! All well dug in and the Russians fought to death in these things. We had to take them out one by one with mines and hand grenades. Those poor Russian devils thought we would finish them off if they surrendered.

The Russia field trip consisted of endless marches. Each time a new horizon loomed up. It drove you crazy. In the evenings we huddled together and chatted. Fortunately, I had quite a few acquaintances at the division, such as Otto Baum and the division's intendant Heinz Lammerding, who had also previously been a pioneer.'

Otto Baum

Bunkers of the Stalin line

'Sturmgeschütz' at the Eastern Front

Ullrich's transfer from 'Totenkopf' to 'Wiking'

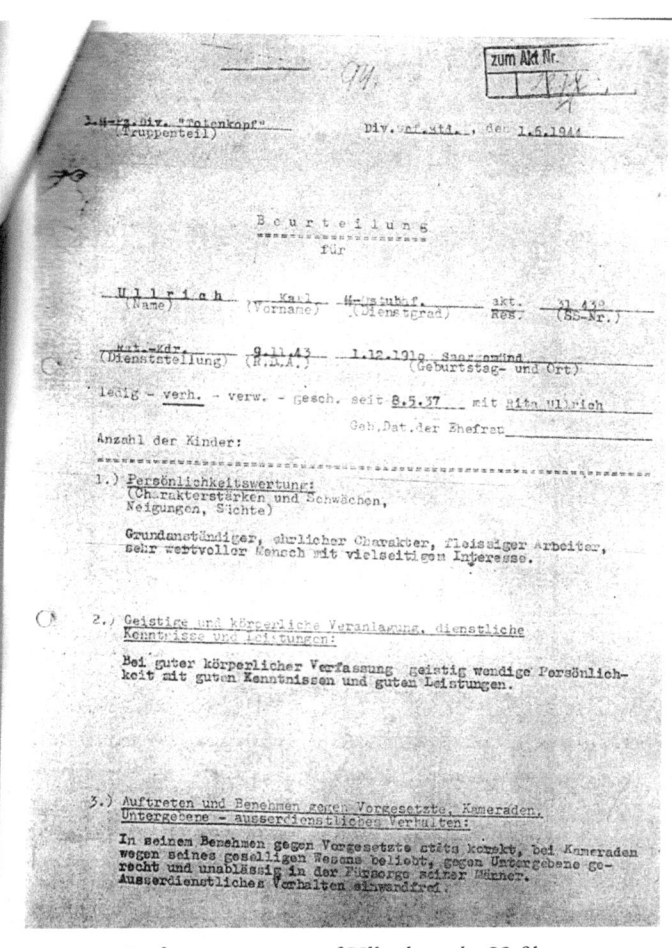

Performance review of Ullrich in the SS files

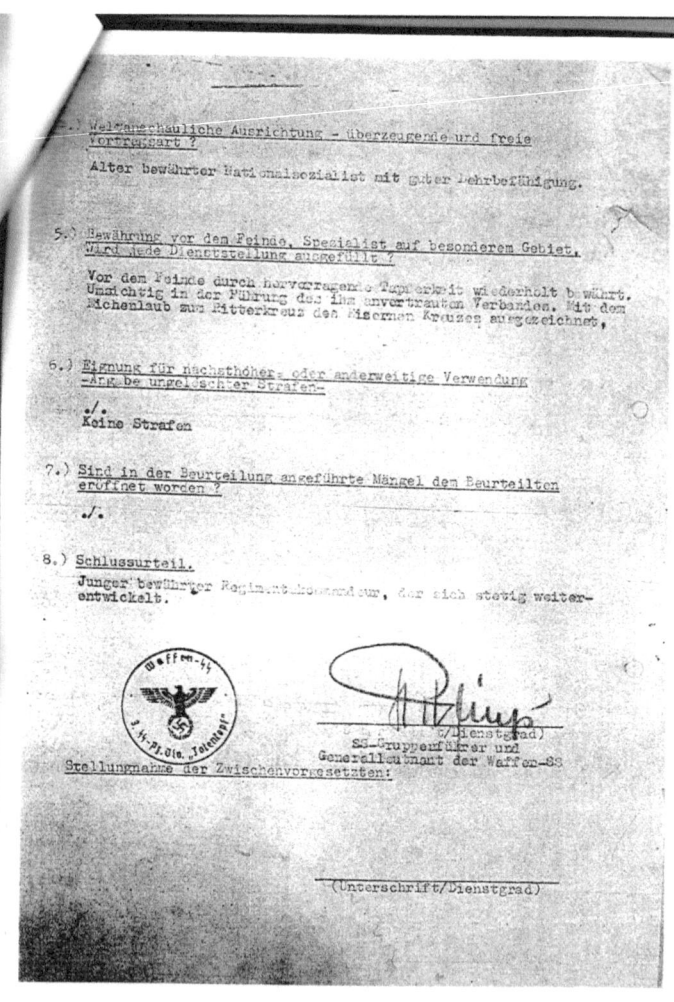

Weltanschauliche Ausrichtung – überzeugende und freie Vortragsart?

Alter bewährter Nationalsozialist mit guter Lehrbefähigung.

5.) Bewährung vor dem Feinde, Spezialist auf besonderem Gebiet. Ward jede Dienststellung ausgefüllt?

Vor dem Feinde durch hervorragende Tapferkeit wiederholt bewährt. Umsichtig in der Führung des ihm unvertrauten Verbandes. Mit dem Eichenlaub zum Ritterkreuz des Eisernen Kreuzes ausgezeichnet.

6.) Eignung für nächsthöhere oder anderweitige Verwendung -Angabe ungelöschter Strafen-

./. Keine Strafen

7.) Sind in der Beurteilung angeführte Mängel dem Beurteilten eröffnet worden?

./.

8.) Schlussurteil.

Junger bewährter Regimentskommandeur, der sich stetig weiterentwickelt.

(Dienstgrad)
SS-Gruppenführer und
Generalleutnant der Waffen-SS

Stellungnahme der Zwischenvorgesetzten:

(Unterschrift/Dienstgrad)

Performance review of Ullrich in the SS files

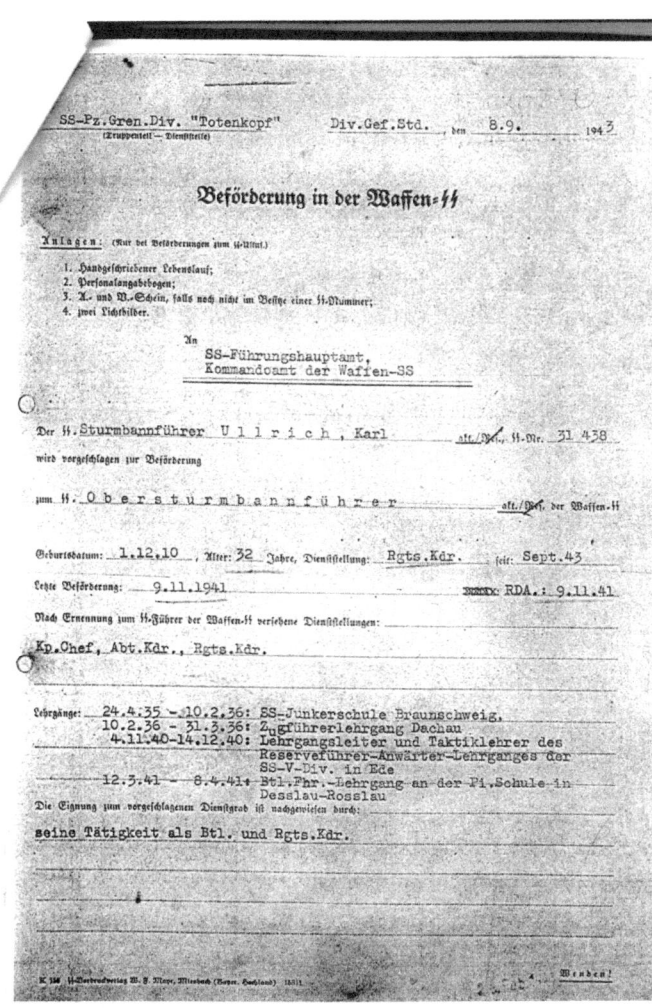

Ullrich's promotion to Obersturmbannführer

...ung der charakterlichen Eignung und dienstlichen Leistungen (Innen- und Außendienst, Lehrfähigkeit, H-Haltung):

SS-Sturmbannführer U l l r i c h hat bereits im Kessel von Demjansk 1942 eine Regimentsgruppe geführt und ist seit kurzem mit der Führung des SS-Pz.Gren.Rgt. "Totenkopf" beauftragt. SS-Stubaf. Ullrich hat sich bisher in allen Lagen als zuverlässiger, umsichtiger und zielbewusster Kommandeur gezeigt. U. besitzt einen lauteren Charakter, ist selbstlos und hart gegen sich.

Teilnahme an Kampfhandlungen: Polenfeldzug, Westfeldzug, Ostfeldzug (1. und 2. Einsatz gegen die Sowjet-Union)

Auszeichnungen: E.K.2.Klasse, E.K.1.Klasse, Ritterkreuz des Eisernen Kreuzes, Sturmabzeichen, Erinnerungs-Medaillen für 13.3.38 und 1.10.38, Spange für Erinnerungs-Med.1.10.38

Zur weiteren Förderung wird ab _____ Verwendung als _____

_____ vorgeschlagen.

Wie oft verwundet ?   —
Verheiratet ?
Alter der Ehefrau ?   ja
Anzahl der Kinder ?

(Unterschrift, Dienstgrad und Dienststellung)
SS-Brigadeführer und
Generalmajor der Waffen-SS

Stellungnahme der vorgesetzten Dienststelle:

Ullrich's promotion to Obersturmbannführer

The campaign brings great successes. Kiev falls, at Rostov follows setback and Moscow and Leningrad remain Russian. South of Leningrad, on the Wolchov River, the foursome of Russian armies launch heavy counterattacks between January and March 1942. An incredibly brutal battle ensues. Symbolic of this are the 15,000 fallen Russians who remain in front of the 'stellungen' of the l26th infantry division after the attack. South of Lake Ilmen, around Demjansk, the German 2nd Army Corps is surrounded by the Red Army. Together with other army units, 'Totenkopf' finds itself in the first 'Kessel' of the Eastern Front. Split into the 'Gruppe Eicke' and the 'Gruppe Simon', named after the officer Max Simon, 'Totenkopf' awaits the Russian attacks.

Ullrich's face tightens. He is visibly struggling to talk about this chapter.

'Demjansk is one of my worst memories. I was with my pioneers in the 'Kessel' and I was with some officers in my 'Gefechtsstand'.
 Ullrich browses through his photo album and shows a small photo. We see a shabby Russian house with a sign in front of it saying 'Ullrich'.

'Yes, here it was,' says Ullrich, continuing his story. 'Suddenly my dog Negus, a nice critter I had scavenged in the Kessel, became nervous. I looked outside and saw at least ten Russian tanks approaching across the snow-covered landscape. I could hear the snow crunching under the tracks. One of the tanks rolled straight towards us and terror struck me. One of my officers crawled out through a hatch and tried to destroy the tank rolling towards us with a 'Teller' mine. He threw it in front of the track but the T-34 rolled past it in the nick of time. The barrel was now turning towards the house and I thought everything was over. But a 'Rottenführer' had meanwhile thrown a mine on the tank and detonated it with a hand grenade. On this I pulled my 'EK-II' off my uniform and pinned the 'Rottenführer' on the chest. He certainly deserved that.'

Shortly afterwards, Ullrich was flown out of the 'Kessel' in a 'Junker-52' transport plane. In the winter of 1942-1943, Ullrich serves as a senior pioneer 'Führer' in Paul Hausser's SS corps. After the failed summer offensive towards Stalingrad and the oil fields of the Caucasus, there is terrible fighting around Kharkov.

'Here we showed Iwan once more that we were his master. But I was no longer at the front but at the map table while the boys of 'Leibstandarte', 'Das Reich' and 'Totenkopf' were in the field. Driving through the field one day with Paul Hausser in his armoured car, I told him I was unhappy with this situation. Hausser understood this and advised me to contact Werner Ostendorff, the 'Chef des Generalstabes' of the corps and apply for another position through him. So I did.

Ostendorff was very kind and said, 'You have seen all sorts of things now why do you not join the infantry?' That seemed a fine idea to me. 'Polizei' for example. But eight days later, Charkov had not yet been completely

Max Simon

Ullrich's headquarters: 'Demjansk is one of my worst memories'

Wounded 'Totenkopf' soldiers

Disabled Soviet tank

Air transport to the surrounded Demjansk

recaptured, a report came in that an officer at 'Totenkopf' had been blinded by an artillery hit. Ostendorff advised me to contact Max Simon, who was in command of 'Totenkopf' after the death of Eicke, who was killed on a reconnaissance flight in a plane. I rang him up and told him I was out of work. In the evening I was already in position with my men. First I commanded a battalion, later a regiment. I experienced the recapture of Kharkov and Bjelgorod.'

In the summer of 1943, the German army definitively loses the initiative in the east during Operation 'Zitadelle' near Kursk. The Allies land on Sicily and the German armies break off the battle of Kursk. From then on, the situation hollows out. It is an endless retreat with heavy losses. 'Totenkopf' is every-

Ullrich with his dog Negus

Summer of 1943, Waffen-SS soldiers with mines at a disabled T-34 tank

'Panther' tank at Kowel, 1944

SS general Herbert Otto Gille, commander of the IV SS.Pz.Corps

where in the important battles of the front, but can the tide of the war be turned around? By the end of 1944, the division was in Poland as part of the IVth SS Armoured Corps of Herbert Otto Gille, a tough and vain officer.

'In the autumn of 1944, I took over command of the 5.SS armoured division 'Wiking'. This was a very special division. Within the framework of 'Wiking', European volunteers fought as part of the crusade against Bolshevism. They came from everywhere - Norway, Finland, Denmark, Belgium, the Netherlands, yes, even Sweden and Switzerland. The division fought mostly together with 'Totenkopf" from 1944 onwards.

Two soldiers who lost their unit are questioned by Ullrich

In January 1945, a new dramatic chapter is added to Ullrich's military experiences. The IVth SS Armoured Corps is transferred from Poland to Hungary. From the vicinity of the Hungarian city of Komorn on the Danube, an offensive is launched towards Budapest. Seventy thousand German and Hungarian soldiers are trapped in Budapest and their only hope is the Waffen-SS corps.

The regimental commander Hans Dorr of the 'Germania' regiment of the 'Wiking' division with the 01. of 'Wiking' Günter Jahnke next to him on the right. Dorr led the 'Wiking' division in Hungary for several days because Ullrich had had a car accident. A true iron fighter, Dorr was wounded nine times and eventually died in Hungary. Jahnke survived the war.

Ullrich understands the garrison's situation; after all, he himself was in Demjansk. However, the German liberation attempt was doomed from the start. On the way to Hungary, Ullrich had a car accident.

Ullrich: 'I was actually lucky, because I got away with nothing. My Ia, an army man, Major Kleine, was injured and had to be replaced.

Nevertheless, I was delayed and therefore I was not there in the early days. The experienced regimental commander Hans Dorr of the regiment 'Germania' was therefore temporarily in command. He later died in Hungary'.

IA Major Kleine with 01. Günter Jahnke

After three eviction attempts, the mission to Budapest finally had to be abandoned. It may have been possible to liberate the garrison but Hitler put a stop to this from a strategic point of view.

The garrison binds troops and so Hitler sacrifices them. On 13 February 1945, Budapest falls. Less than seven hundred soldiers manage to break out.

'In March, the last major and by history totally forgotten German offensive began: 'Frühlingserwachen'. By then 'Wiking' was totally exhausted and was in defensive positions around Stuhlweissenburg. After ten days of a small German advance through the mud landscape, the Red Army attacked. North of us, including 'Totenkopf', everything was mowed away and hardly anything

Soldier with 'Panzerfaust'

Waffen-SS sniper

Waffen-SS soldier, Demjansk

remained. To make matters worse, the 'Führerbefehl' came to preserve the town of Stuhlweissenburg (Székesfehérvar) as a 'Festung'. This would be our end. Everyone was aware that Budapest was lost and all the soldiers wanted to go west. Finally, a radio call came in from Gille telling us to break out. I did. General Breith of the 3rd Armoured Corps, a pleasant man, later covered for me.'

'The last few days were horrible. I even had to deploy my personal armoured vehicle because everything else had been destroyed. During the retreat, one of my best officers, Fritz Vogt, former commander of the Noren battalion, was badly wounded. I rushed to him. When I was with him he expressed his regret that he had never received the 'Eichenlaub'. On this I took mine and pinned it on him. He was very happy and died shortly afterwards. I myself narrowly escaped death a few days later. Suddenly we encountered Russian armoured vehicles. In my long leather jacket, I was not very fast and I dove into my armoured vehicle.

Operation 'Frühlingserwachen', disabled 'Jagdpanther' at Dég

The 01. of 'Wiking', Günter Jahnke, married Ullrich's sister after the war

On the right, the regiment commander, Hans Dorr, of regiment 'Germania' of the 'Wiking' division with the 01. of the 'Wiking' Günter Jahnke next to him. Dorr led the 'Wiking' division for serveral days in Hungary because Ullrich had been in a car accident. Dorr was real go-getter and was wounded nine times before he finally fell in Hungary. Jahnke survived the war

Herbert Otto Gille, commander of the IV SS-armoured corps

Captivity in Regensburg

The bullets were whizzing around my ears. My adjutant was shot through both legs. I was lucky again. We crossed the Austro-Hungarian border and subsequently fell into American captivity. Despite the fact that we had never fought in the West, they knew the division. The war was over and I disappeared into captivity for several years.'

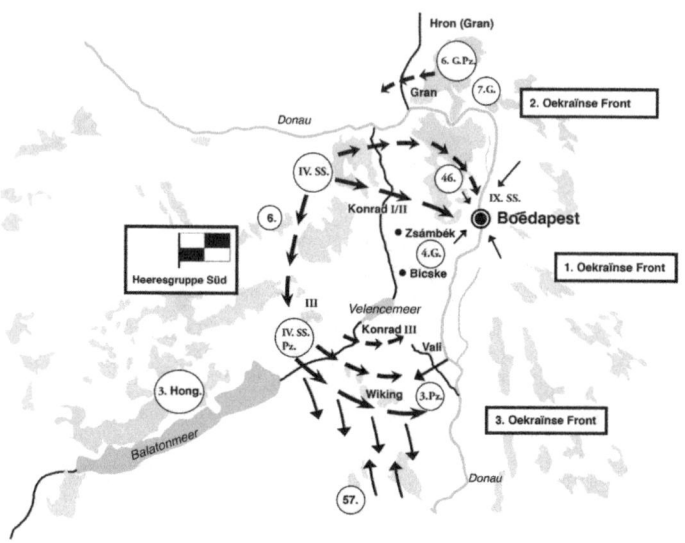

Hungary, January 1945

My Homeland

'I fought at the front for my homeland for almost six years. And after the war, what was the appreciation for this? Nothing at all. At least from the state. It looked at us as if we were criminals. We were not. We were soldiers. Good soldiers. However, the German state blindly adopted world opinion, which put its stamp on us. That is why we have to be quiet now. At least you Dutch have a homeland. We Germans do not. That is tragic. Our political leadership is worthless. Just look at the 'Grünen'. What idiots they are with their grey socks and sandals. Are they supposed to rule our country? But I cannot say anything. I must keep quiet. It is useless to say anything.

In a hundred years, everyone will speak positively about us. Now we can only remain correct and work diligently. And above all, keep our mouths shut. Stay calm. Despise is too strong a word for how I feel about Germany.

How do I best express myself? Germany has orderly workers, sure, but no political leadership. Germany lacks a strong man. For a country to lead the whole world, it must have a strong leader.

Recently, there has been too much talk about the right-wing radical Franz Schönhuber of the 'Republikaner' party. I know him and his kind. He does not belong with us. I saw it right away when I read his first book. Schönhuber is nothing at all. There is really nothing in it at all. He was in the Waffen-SS for fourteen days and already had a soa. Yes, chasing chicks, that he can do. It will be nothing with Schönhuber. He cannot give the marching order.

Franz Josef Strauss, the Bavarian party leader of the CSU, I met many a time. He was an honest politician. However, we should not drag on about him. Look around you: it is your generation's turn. All the politicians who make it are between 30 and 50. We do not count anymore. We must remain calm. If there are questions, we will answer.

The political leadership in Germany may not have accepted us but German society did. Never before have I been attacked by a fellow German citizen who resented my Waffen-SS past. Never before. After my three years of captivity, I joined Lammerding in Düsseldorf. I still knew Lammerding from the 'Junkerschule' in Braunschweig. He had his own company. I was engineer there. They were all people from 'us' there. One time I came to a construction site and one of the workers says: 'Hey, Standartenführer, how are you?' Nobody ripped off my awards. I am even an honorary member of an association for knight's cross bearers. Yet the political leadership has not accepted our kind of people. That arouses indignation. I will tell you that in a hundred years, the Third Reich will be appreciated quite differently. Admittedly, Hitler will not become as popular as Napoleon. But still, just watch! Therefore, if I had to redo my life from 1910, I would do exactly the same as I did.'

Karl Ullrich's Life in a Nutshell

Born 1 December 1910 in Saargemünd
1921-1927 Realschule in Bad Kissingen
1933 Examination mechanical engineer
1933 Volunteer with infantry regiment 19, education at Truppenübungsplatz Grafenwöhr
1934 Service SS-Verfügungstruppe and member of 7.Hundertschaft of the Landespolizei München
July 1934 Petty officer in the SS-Standarte 1, Munich
March 1935 Officer training Junkerschule Braunschweig
1936 SS-Pioniersbataillon in Leisnig
1936 Heerespionierschule Dessau-Rohlau
1 September 1937 SS-Obersturmführer, commander 3.compagnie SS-Pioniersturmbann
1938 Chief. 3.Pio.company
Participation Anschluss Austria
Entry Sudetenland
1939 Poland field trip. Commander SS pioneer unit, operating within an army unit
1940 Field trip in the west within the SS-Verfügungs division (Netherlands and France)
1940 Eiseren Kreuz award I and II
1941 Yugoslavia field trip

May 1941 transfer to the SS-Totenkopf division
1941 Commander of SS-Pionierbataillon 3
June-July 1941 Breakthrough Stalin Line, Russia Conquest
January 1942 defensive fighting in area around Waldai and Staraja Russa (surrounded, together with the 18th infantry division (mot.)
February 1942 Fighting near Kobylkina, breakout
to the 'Gruppe Eicke', Ritterkreuz for Ullrich.
Summer 1942 Korpspionierführer
Winter Charkov
March 1943 takes command of III. Battalion SS- Panzergrenadierregiment 5 'Totenkopf' takes over from SS-Sturmbannführer Joachim Schubach
July 1943 battles at Pssel as part of Battle of
Kursk
November 1943 SS-Obersturmbannführer
10 November 1943 commander of SS-panzergrenadierregiment 6 'Theodor Eicke'
November 1943 fighting around Bairak
March 1944 retreat fighting and defence, among others around Ljubomirka
14 May 1944 Eichenlaub zum Ritterkreuz as 480th soldier
29 July 1944 SS-Standartenführer
9 October 1944 appointed commander of the
5th SS-Panzerdivision 'Wiking'
November-December 1944 defence front around
Warsaw, Modlin
December 1944 transport to Hungary
January 1945 attempt to relieve German-Hungarian

garrison of Budapest. Attack in mountain area (Pilisge-mountains)

18 January 1945, new attempt to relieve Budapest north of Lake Balaton

February 1945 defensive battles around Stuhlweissenburg

6 March 1945 deployment within operation 'Frühlingserwachen', offensive 6th SS Armoured Army in Hungary

16 March 1945, Start Vienna operation of Red Army. 'Wiking' is ordered to hold Stuhlweissenburg, but breaks out to the west

April-May 1945 defensive battles in the Steiermark

20 April 1945 SS-Oberführer

12 May 1945 in US captivity at Radstadt

18 September 1948 discharge from captivity

1984 Ullrich publishes with Munin-Verlag his division history of the 'Totenkopf' division, *Wie ein Fels im Meer.*

8 May 1996 death anniversary of Karl Ullrich

Literature

Boog/Förster/Hoffmann/Klink/Müller/Ueberschar, Der Angriff auf die Sowjetunion (Frankfurt am Main 1991)

Broekmeyer, M., Stalin de Russen en hun oorlog 1941-1945 (Amsterdam 1999)

Die Wehrmachtberichte 1939-1945. (band 1) (Munich 1985)

Dumas, Y, De stalen vuist van de Blitzkrieg. De 1ste Panzer Division 1939-1941 (Soesterberg 2013)

Glantz, D.M., The initial Period of War on the Eastern Front 22 June-August 1941 (London 1993)

Oetting, D.W., Verbrannte Erde. Kein Krieg wie im Westen: Wehrmacht und Sowjetarmee im Russlandkrieg 1941-1945. (Graz 2011)

Overy, R., Ruslands oorlog. (Soesterberg 2005)

Pierik, P., De geopolitiek van het Derde Rijk (Soesterberg 2013)

Pierik, P., Het onbekende Reich. Minder bekende feiten van het oostfront. (Soesterberg 2014)

Pierik, P., De zwarte magiër. Karl Haushofer, zijn invloed op Hitler en de kruistocht voor 'Lebensraum'. (Soesterberg 2015)

Strassner, P., Die 5. SS Panzerdivision Wiking (1969)

Tessin, G ., Verbände und Truppen der deutschen Wehrmacht und Waffen-SS im Zweiten Weltkrieg (Osnabrück 1975)

Ullrich, K., Wie ein Fels im Meer, 3. SS Panzerdivision 'Totenkopf' (1984)

Warlimont, W., Imm Hauptquartier der deutschen Wehrmacht 1939-1945. Grundlagen Formen, Gestalten. band I (1990)

Thanks to mr. Mirko Bayerl for the use of some pictures.